# THE STORY OF HARRIET TUBMAN

**A Biography Book for New Readers**

By
**CHRISTINE PLATT**

Illustrations by
**LORIS LORA**

ROCKRIDGE PRESS

**For Harriet's sister, Rachel Ross, and her children, Ben and Angerine.**



For general information on our other products and services or to obtain technical support, please contact our Customer Care Department within the United States at (866) 744-2665, or outside the United States at (510) 253-0500.

Rockridge Press publishes its books in a variety of electronic and print formats. Some content that appears in print may not be available in electronic books, and vice versa.



Art Director and Cover Lettering: Jane Archer

Art Producer: Hillary Frileck

Editor: Kristen Depken

Production Manager: Jose Olivera

Production Editor: Melissa Edeburn

Illustration © 2020 Loris Lora.

Creative Market/Mia Buono, pp 2, 11, 27, 34, 37.

Author photo © Norman E. Jones Photography.

Illustrator photo © Sam Kimbrell.

ISBN: 978-1-64611-109-1 | eBook 978-1-64611-110-7

Ro

Printed in China

# CONTENTS


CHAPTER 1 A Leader Is Born 1

CHAPTER 2 The Early Years 9

CHAPTER 3 No Longer a Child 16

CHAPTER 4 Freedom Is Calling 22

CHAPTER 5 Liberty for All! 30

CHAPTER 6 General Tubman 37

CHAPTER 7 More Work to Be Done 44

CHAPTER 8 So . . . Who Was Harriet Tubman? 51

GLOSSARY 58

BIBLIOGRAPHY 60

# CHAPTER 1

# A LEADER IS BORN

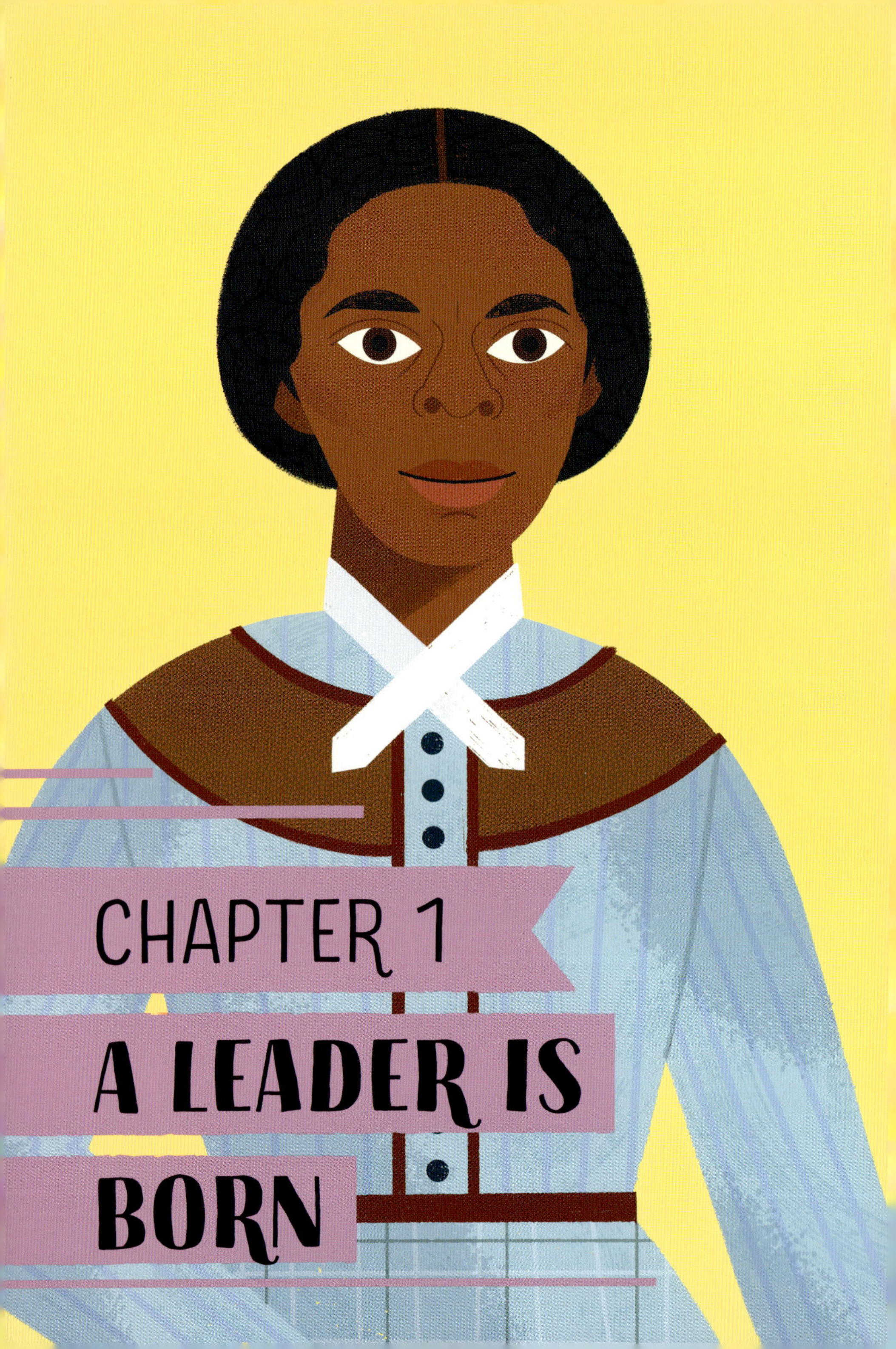

# Meet Harriet Tubman

Araminta Ross wasn't the type of child people imagined would grow up to become a leader. In fact, Araminta was born with many odds against her. Surprisingly, her biggest challenge would be the reason she became known as the brave leader, Harriet Tubman. That's because she was born into a life of **slavery**.

Araminta's journey to become Harriet Tubman wasn't easy. Her entire family was **enslaved**. As a child, she saw her parents and siblings struggle as they worked on a **plantation**. Because Araminta's family members were **slaves**, they didn't receive pay for the hard work they were forced to do. When Araminta was just five years old, she was forced to work as well.

As Araminta grew older, she became determined to free herself and her family from slavery forever. On her journey in search of freedom, Araminta grew from a young slave girl into the courageous woman Harriet Tubman.

Harriet spent much of her life helping other **enslaved people** gain their freedom as well. She put herself in danger countless times to help others. Harriet even served as a spy during the American Civil War. When Harriet became known for her brave acts, she used her fame to help even more people. So how did Harriet's amazing story begin?

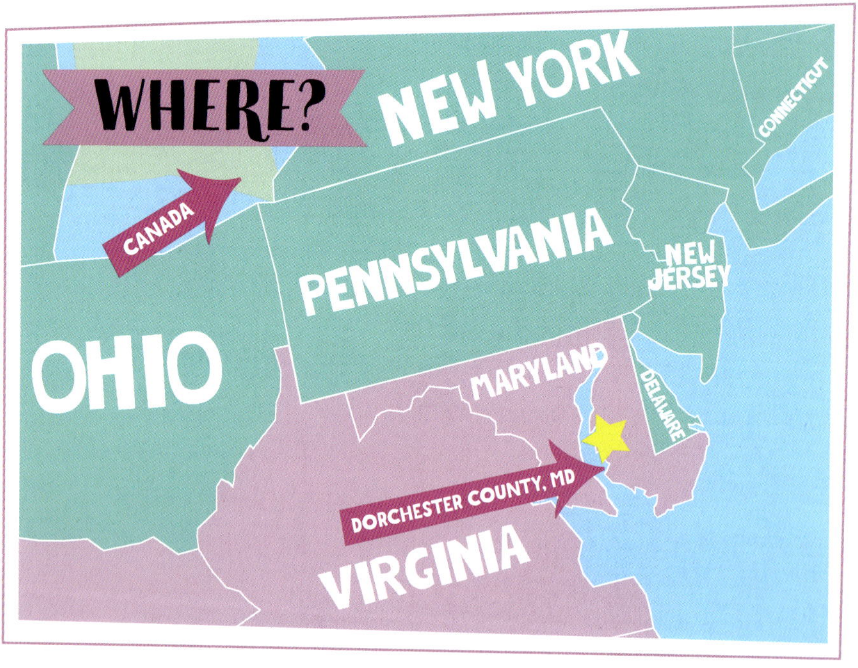

## Harriet's America

Around 1822, Harriet Green and Benjamin Ross had their fifth child, a daughter named Araminta Ross—who would grow up to become known as the hero Harriet Tubman.

Historians believe Araminta was born on a plantation in Dorchester County, Maryland. The exact date and location of her birth isn't known because she was born enslaved. Araminta was often called by her nickname—Minty. She was one of the many **descendants** of African people who were captured and sold into slavery in the Americas, the Caribbean, and many British colonies. Enslaved people were considered property. The Brodess family owned Minty's parents, which meant they also owned Minty.

Because Minty's parents were enslaved, they couldn't afford to buy her presents. But Minty's father was a good carpenter, and he made a wooden cradle for his newborn daughter.

## American Slavery

Slavery was a system in which some people were forced to work on plantations **harvesting** crops. Other enslaved people were forced to cook, clean, and take care of their owners' homes and children. In America, white people of European **ancestry** mainly used black people of African ancestry as slave labor. Enslaved black people were considered property and were often treated very poorly. Enslaved people were not paid for their work, and **slave owners** often sold them to other plantations, which separated families. By 1804, the Northern states had ended slavery, so most enslaved people worked on plantations in the South. People who escaped slavery and ran away to the North were considered free. Many people tried to escape, but those slaves who were captured and returned to their slave owners were badly punished, sometimes even killed.

Minty's mother was one of the Brodess family's house slaves. She had to cook their meals. Minty's father was a woodworker on the plantation. He was often forced to do woodwork for neighbors, too.

**MYTH & FACT**

**MYTH:** Black people willingly came to America to work as slaves.

**FACT:** They were captured in Africa and sold into slavery. Over time, very few people of African ancestry knew their true origins. Those who did had no way to return—America was the only home they'd ever known.

Enslaved peoples' lives were very difficult. Forced to work long hours, they were punished if they did not do what their owners demanded. Many slave owners were very cruel—they used whips and canes to beat their slaves. So, most slaves did as they were told out of fear. They were afraid of what would happen to them if they disobeyed or tried to escape to the North.

Before Minty was five years old, she did not have to work as a slave. Still, she saw the long hours her parents, siblings, and other enslaved people worked. Minty also saw her loved ones and other people being mistreated. As she grew older, Minty was determined not to spend her entire life in slavery.

## WHEN?

**1619** — The first enslaved Africans arrive in Jamestown, Virginia.

**1776** — American colonies declare independence from Britain.

**BEFORE 1790** — Harriet's grandmother is sold into slavery in Maryland.

**1804** — Last Northern state abolishes slavery, but it continues in the South.

**AROUND 1822** — Araminta "Minty" Ross is born.

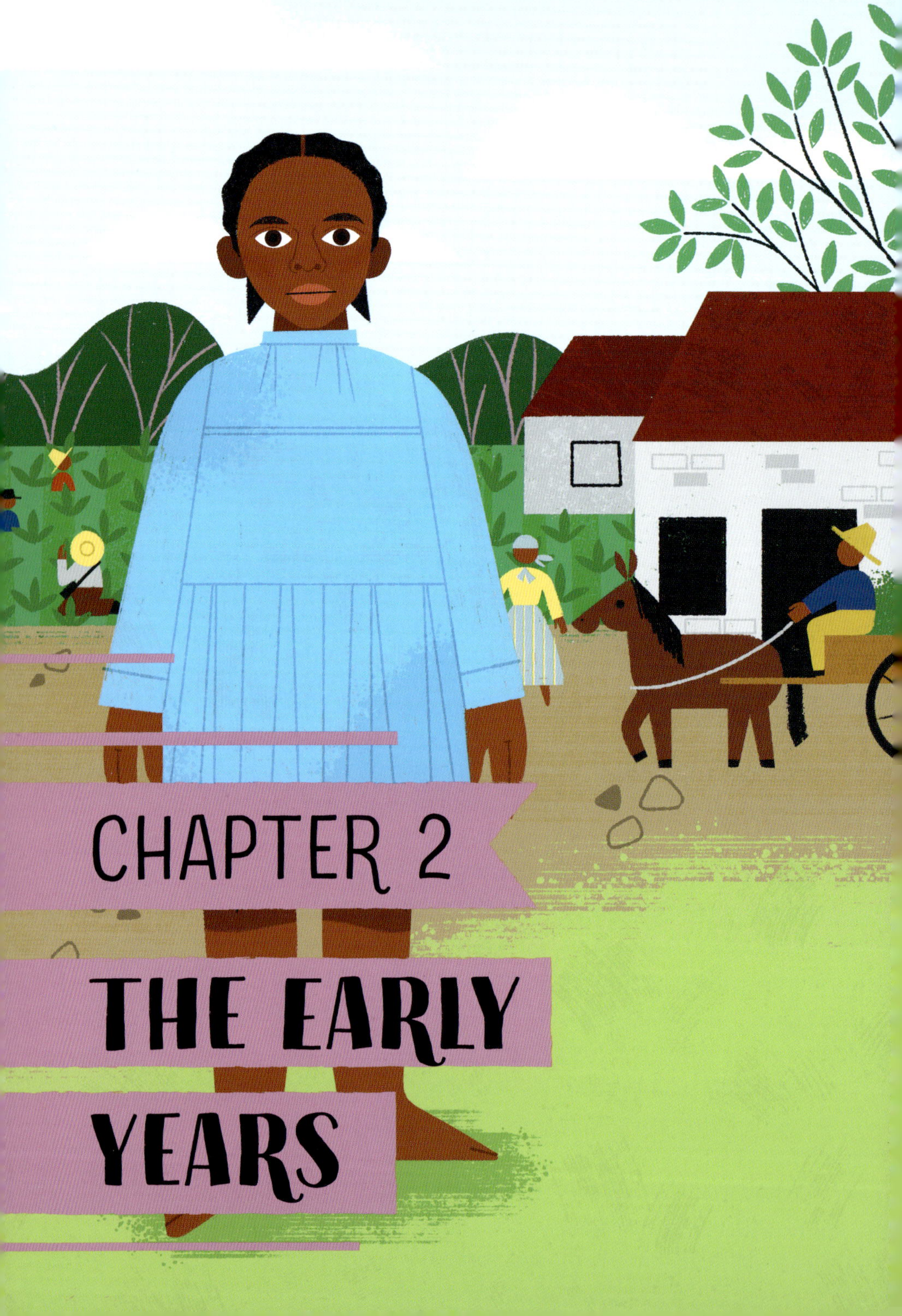

# CHAPTER 2
# THE EARLY YEARS

# Growing Up in Slavery

Enslaved people who were forced to harvest crops were known as "field slaves." Field slaves had to work outside for hours in the hot sun. Enslaved people who worked in the home were known as "house slaves." Their work wasn't easy, but it was considered better than working in the fields.

Minty's mother hoped Mr. Brodess would make her daughter a house slave. She didn't want Minty to have a difficult life in the field. But even though Minty was her daughter, Minty was considered the property of the Brodess family. Mr. Brodess would decide Minty's fate.

Minty didn't go to school. It was considered a crime for enslaved people to learn how to read or write. But like many slaves, Minty's parents memorized the Bible stories told at church.

Minty loved it when her mother told her Bible stories. Minty devoted her life to serving God as a young girl. Soon, she could recite Bible stories and long scriptures by memory.

As Minty grew older, her father taught her about nature by taking her outside.

## Family Tree

Minty learned about many types of trees and plants. Minty loved it most when she and her father went outside at night.

Together, they'd look up at the night sky as Minty's father explained the starry patterns. He was the first person to tell Minty about the North Star—the brightest star in the sky. He told her that people who wanted to escape slavery followed the North Star to freedom.

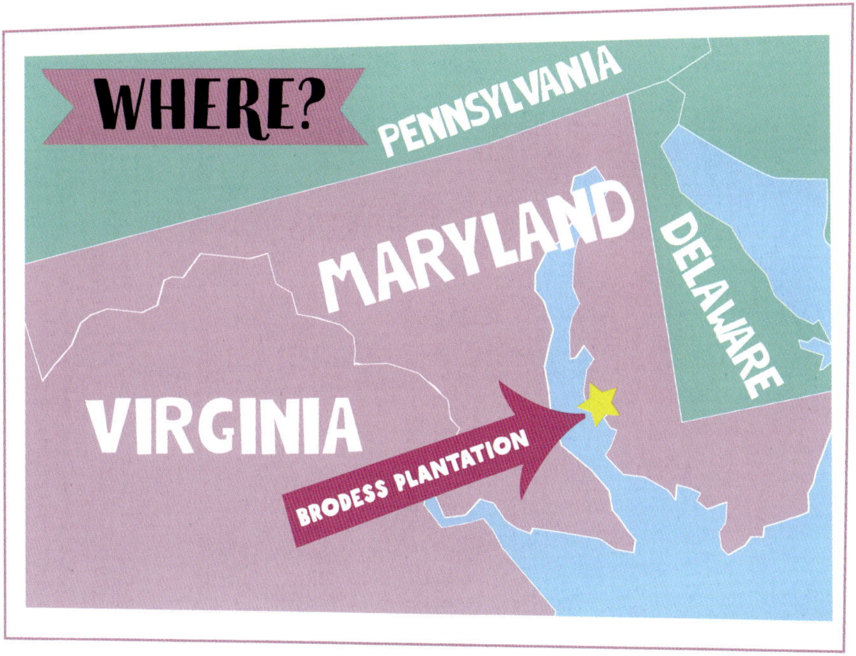

**MYTH & FACT**

**MYTH:** Only enslaved adults were forced to work on plantations.

**FACT:** Children as young as five years old were also used as slave labor.

## Put to Work

Minty was five or six years old when Mr. Brodess decided it was time for her first job. He sent her to work for the Cook family. She would check their muskrat traps. The Cooks were mean. Whenever they thought Minty wasn't doing a good job, they beat her. Once, Minty caught the measles and became very ill. But the Cooks thought Minty was just being lazy, and they told Mr. Brodess they no longer wanted her to work for them.

Next, Mr. Brodess sent Minty to work for his neighbor, Miss Susan. She was a new mother and used Minty as a babysitter. Minty watched, changed, and fed Miss Susan's baby. But Miss Susan never wanted to hear her baby crying. It was an impossible task—all babies cry. Whenever Miss Susan heard her baby fussing, Minty was punished.

## JUMP IN THE THINK TANK

How would you feel if you were sent away from your family to work for strangers every day?

Minty didn't like how Miss Susan treated her, but she thought her home was lovely. Minty liked to go from room to room and look at Miss

Susan's fancy things. One day, Minty saw sugar cubes in the kitchen. She took one. It was a big mistake—Miss Susan was watching her.

Enslaved people who were caught stealing, even something as small as a sugar cube, were punished. When Minty realized Miss Susan had seen her, she ran and hid inside a pigpen where no one could find her. But Minty knew she couldn't hide forever. After five days, she returned to face her punishment and was beaten so badly that she almost died. When Minty got better, Mr. Brodess sent her to work in the fields.

## WHEN?

Araminta "Minty" Ross is born.

**AROUND 1822**

Minty begins working as a slave.

**ABOUT 1827**

# CHAPTER 3

# NO LONGER A CHILD

## Hard Work

Minty quickly discovered that being a field slave was much harder than checking the Cooks' muskrat traps and babysitting for Miss Susan. Every day, Minty worked in the hot sun. Mr. Brodess hired an **overseer** to watch field slaves harvesting crops. If the overseer saw Minty or anyone else resting or working too slowly, he would punish them.

Harvesting tobacco was hard work for Minty. Minty did as she was told so the overseer wouldn't think she was being lazy. She hated watching the overseer beat other people for working too slowly. Being in the field made Minty long for her freedom even more.

In the summer of 1831, Minty learned that an enslaved man named Nat Turner tried to escape from a plantation in Virginia. Maryland slave owners like the Brodesses were worried because Nat didn't just run away—he started a **rebellion**.

After Nat killed his owner and freed himself, he freed other enslaved people on the plantation. Then, Nat asked for their help to free as many enslaved people as possible. Together, they went to other plantations, killed dozens of white slave owners, and freed more people. Eventually, Nat and those who helped him were captured. But after such a deadly rebellion, many slave owners feared the same thing could happen on their plantations.

Minty knew she could never kill Mr. Brodess. But she was curious about another way she had heard people escaped slavery—the Underground Railroad.

As Minty grew older, she continued to dream of freedom for herself and other enslaved people. When Minty was around 12 years old, a slave tried to escape the Brodesses' plantation and was captured. While he was being punished, Minty tried to protect him. Sadly, Minty was struck in the head with such force that she almost died.

## MYTH & FACT

**MYTH:** The Underground Railroad was a train system.

**FACT:** It was a secret route of safe places to help enslaved people escape to the North and Canada. The homes, barns, and churches on the Underground Railroad were owned by free black people and white people who disagreed with slavery.

Minty's wounds eventually healed, but she wasn't the same as before. She had terrible "sleeping spells" that caused her to pass out without warning. Because Minty could no longer work in the fields, Mr. Brodess gave her different tasks to do around the plantation. But she still wasn't free.

## Strong Mind

Minty believed her sleeping spells made her mind stronger than it was before her injury and that God now spoke to her through her dreams.

> "In my dreams and visions, I seemed to see a line, and on the other side of that line were green fields, and lovely flowers."

Minty often dreamed she was talking to angels about escaping slavery. Soon, Minty would need her strong mind to do important work for her people.

## WHEN?

Nat Turner's Rebellion takes place in Virginia.

**AUGUST 1831**

Minty is injured trying to protect another slave.

**AROUND 1834**

# CHAPTER 4
# FREEDOM IS CALLING

## From Minty to Harriet Tubman

When Minty was a young woman, she changed her name. She thought "Minty" sounded too childlike for someone who had survived so much. She renamed herself Harriet in honor of her mother.

When Harriet was hired out to chop timber for a shipyard owner named John Stewart around 1840, she worked extra hard. Sometimes, Mr. Stewart had money left over after he'd paid Mr. Brodess for Harriet's work. Whenever he gave Harriet the extra money, she saved it. When the time came for Harriet to escape, she knew she would need it.

In 1844, Harriet met John Tubman, a free black man. He asked Harriet to marry him. Even though John was free, he didn't have the same rights and **privileges** as white men.

Harriet would be his wife, but she would still be considered the property of Mr. Brodess. If John and Harriet had children, their children would become the property of Mr. Brodess as well.

## JUMP IN THE THINK TANK

How would you feel if your loved one was someone else's property?

Despite these challenges, Harriet agreed to marry John. When Harriet was around 25 years old, she became Mrs. Harriet Tubman. She sewed a beautiful quilt to honor their union.

Harriet continued to dream about escaping slavery. One day, Harriet told John about her visions. Rather than support her, John said he would turn her in if she tried to escape. Harriet never spoke to him about her dreams again.

## Escape to Freedom!

In 1849, Harriet heard that Mr. Brodess planned to sell some of his slaves and send them farther south, where slavery was much worse. Harriet was terrified. She prayed that Mr. Brodess would change his mind.

> "I prayed all night long for my master till the first of March."

Mr. Brodess didn't change his mind, so Harriet changed her prayer: "Oh Lord, if you ain't never going to change that man's heart, kill him, Lord, and take him out of the way."

When Mr. Brodess died a week later, Harriet

felt guilty and afraid. No one knew what would happen next. Harriet's sisters, Linah, Soph, and Mariah, had been sold a few years before. Harriet didn't want that to happen to her brothers, Henry and Ben. She came up with a plan to use the Underground Railroad to escape. On September 17, 1849, Harriet, Ben, and Henry fled into the night.

Harriet was excited to finally start the journey north, just as she'd always dreamed. But along the way, Henry and Ben became afraid. Harriet tried to convince them to continue their trip, but they decided to return to the Brodesses' Poplar Neck Plantation. Harriet went with them to make sure they got back safely.

But Harriet didn't stay for long. Two days later, she gathered her money, a small amount of food, and her wedding quilt. She escaped alone. Just as her father had taught her, Harriet followed the North Star as her guide.

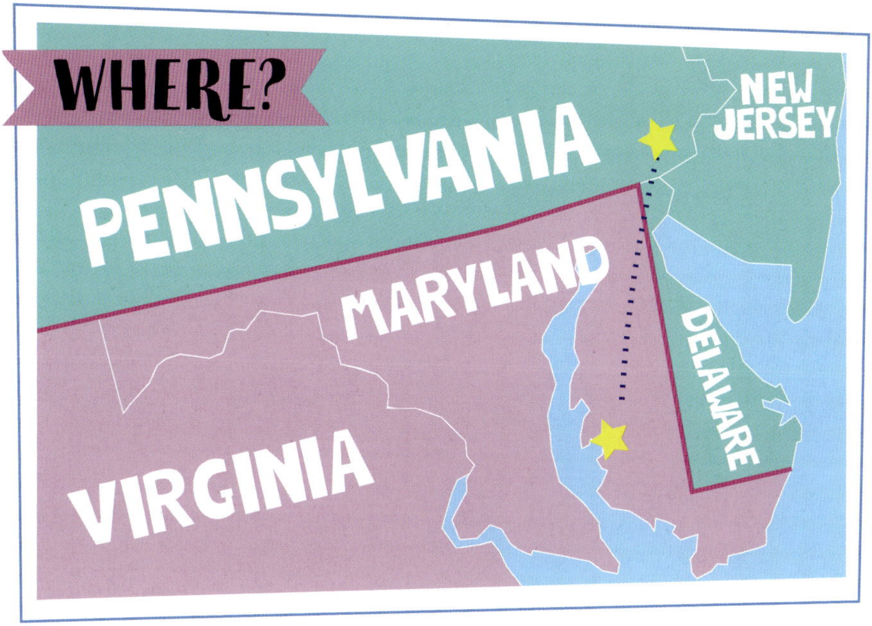


Some people were willing to help anyone trying to escape slavery. These people left items like lit lanterns outside their homes along the secret route of the Underground Railroad. Harriet saw one of these lanterns outside the home of a **Quaker** woman, who let Harriet come inside and rest. She then told Harriet how to get to the next safe house. Harriet was so grateful that she gave the woman her wedding quilt in thanks.

## MYTH & FACT

**MYTH:** Running away was an easy way to escape.

**FACT:** It was very dangerous. Many people who ran away returned out of fear.

Over several days, many other kind and brave people helped Harriet travel north. After she walked nearly 90 miles, she finally crossed the border into Pennsylvania. Harriet was free! She promised to one day return to Poplar Neck to free her family as well.

## WHEN?

**AROUND 1840** — Harriet begins working to chop timber for John Stewart.

**1844** — Harriet marries John Tubman.

**1849** — Harriet runs away from Poplar Neck Plantation.

# CHAPTER 5

# LIBERTY FOR ALL!

## An Underground Conductor

From the moment she crossed into Pennsylvania, Harriet loved the feeling of freedom.

> "When I found I had crossed that line, I looked at my hands to see if I was the same person. There was such a **glory** over everything; the sun came like **gold** through the trees, and over the fields, and I felt **like I was in Heaven.**"

With the help of the Pennsylvania Vigilance Committee, Harriet went to Philadelphia. The committee helped people who escaped slavery find jobs and keep in touch with their family members who were still enslaved. Its chairman, Mr. William Still, helped Harriet find work as a maid. Harriet saved every dollar she earned. She planned to use the money to rescue her family.

One day, Harriet found out that her niece, Kessiah, and her two children, James and Araminta, were about to be sold. Harriet returned to Maryland. She hid in a safe house until Kessiah and her children could meet her. Then, Harriet used the Underground Railroad to lead them all to freedom. For Harriet, it was the first of many trips.

## Moses of Her People

Harriet continued to travel to help free more of her family members and close friends. Then

Congress passed a law that made Harriet's work even more dangerous.

The Fugitive Slave Law of 1850 said people who escaped slavery and who were found in the North could be returned to their former owners in the South. Anyone who helped people escape slavery could be jailed, fined, or worse. Slave owners heard about Harriet and offered large rewards for anyone who captured her.

Even though she had to be more careful now, Harriet continued to risk her life to free people. She wore **disguises**, and she often dressed and acted like an old woman to appear harmless. Harriet helped so many people escape that her nickname was Moses, like the man in the Bible who led his people to freedom.

Harriet asked her husband to join her in Philadelphia. She knew his life would be better if he lived in a free state. But Harriet learned that John had already married another woman.

Harriet continued her work and acted like a **conductor** for the Underground Railroad. She had one rule: Any person who joined her on the trip north could not turn back. Because of this rule, Harriet never lost a single passenger.

Because people who escaped slavery and who were caught in the North could be returned to their slave owners in the South, Harriet started taking people all the way to Canada. Slavery was

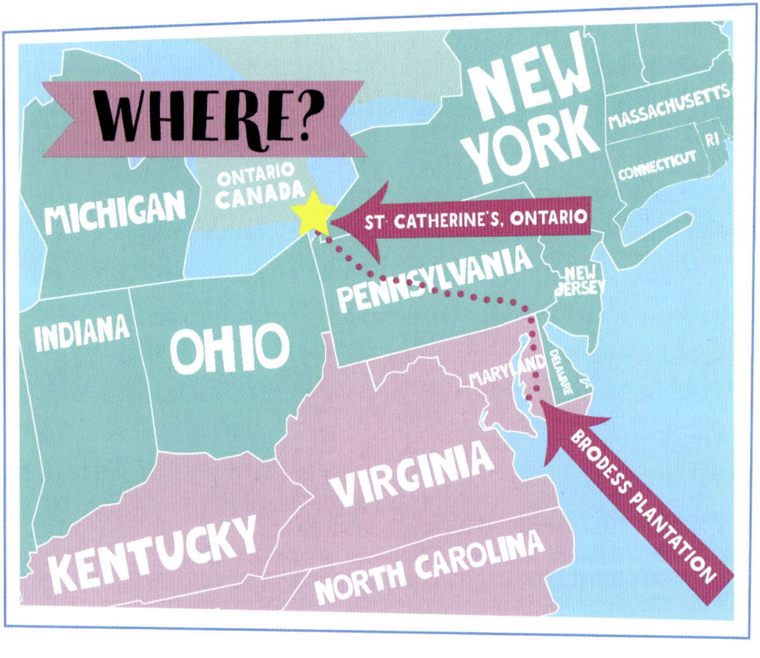

no longer legal in Canada, and that country had no Fugitive Slave Law. Many former slaves started a community in St. Catharines, Ontario. Harriet helped many people, including her elderly parents and brothers, escape to St. Catharines.

Harriet had fulfilled her promise to free her loved ones and others from the horrors of slavery.

## JUMP IN THE THINK TANK

Most slaves who escaped to freedom never returned to the South because it was so dangerous. Harriet was very brave. Do you think you could have been as brave?

## WHEN?

| 1849 | 1850 | 1851 |
|---|---|---|
| Harriet escapes using the Underground Railroad. | The Fugitive Slave Law is passed. | Harriet begins leading slaves to freedom in Canada. |

# CHAPTER 6
# GENERAL TUBMAN

## Saving Charles Nalle

In time, Harriet set up a house for her family in Auburn, New York. It was wonderful for them to be together again. But Harriet's work wasn't finished.

Many people remained trapped in slavery. Harriet could not save everyone, but she often gave speeches about the need to **abolish** slavery.

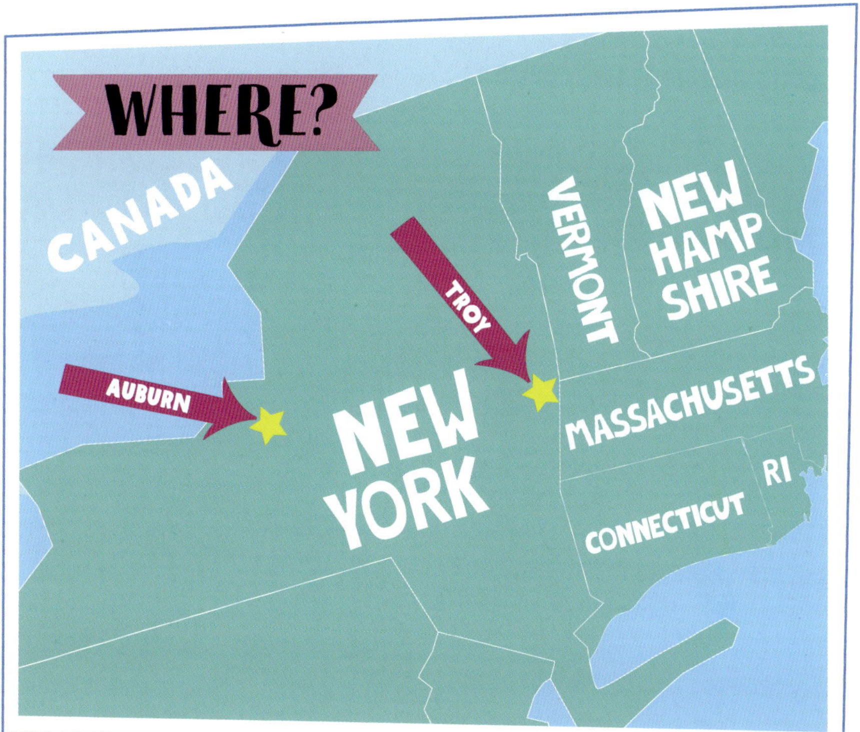

Because Harriet was so popular, she was paid to speak at events. Harriet always saved her money to continue her important work.

Sometimes, Harriet's work came to her by surprise. On April 27, 1860, Harriet was visiting Troy, New York, when she learned that a former slave named Charles Nalle had been captured while looking for his wife, and their children. Harriet disguised herself as an old woman,

found Charles, and helped him get away. Others helped him escape to a nearby city.

But Charles wasn't safe yet. Slave catchers tracked him and captured him again. This time, Harriet and others stormed the building in which he was being held. They freed Charles once again, this time for good.

### JUMP IN THE THINK TANK

Can you imagine how angry slave owners and slave catchers were at Harriet for freeing so many people?

When slave owners heard that Harriet had helped rescue Charles Nalle, they were furious. They increased the **bounty** for anyone who captured her. Harriet's family and friends were worried for her safety. They convinced her to stop using the Underground Railroad, but Harriet soon found another way to help.

## A Respected Leader

America's Civil War began on April 12, 1861. Northern states that wanted to end slavery formed the Union Army. Southern states that wanted to keep enslaving people formed the Confederate Army. Many enslaved and freed black men served in the Union Army. Some women, like Harriet, served as well.

The Governor of Massachusetts, John A. Andrew, was an **abolitionist**. He knew that, because of her work, Harriet was very familiar with the **terrain** of the South. He asked her to help Union troops there.

> "Harriet, you are to act as a spy, scout, or nurse, as the circumstances require."
>
> —*Massachusetts Governor* JOHN A. ANDREW

Harriet said yes and was sent to South Carolina, where she worked as a nurse and spied on Confederate soldiers. She also served as a **liaison** between Union soldiers and enslaved people. Soon, Harriet was so respected in the Union Army, she became Commander of Intelligence Operations for the Union Army's Department of the South. Nine men served under Harriet's command.

One of Harriet's biggest successes was in 1863, when she led some 150 black Union Army soldiers along the Combahee River in South Carolina to rescue more than 700 slaves.

**MYTH & FACT**

**MYTH:** Only men joined the Union Army.

**FACT:** More than 400 women served in the Union Army as soldiers, nurses, and cooks, and in other occupations.

Harriet's service ended in 1865, when the Union Army defeated the Confederate Army. All enslaved people in America were soon given their freedom.

## WHEN?

| 1860 | 1861 | 1865 |
|---|---|---|
| Harriet helps Charles Nalle escape slave catchers. | The American Civil War begins. | Slavery is abolished in America. |

# CHAPTER 7
# MORE WORK TO BE DONE

## One Big Family

When the Civil War ended, Harriet was grateful—black people were finally free. Harriet went home to Auburn, New York, to care for her elderly parents. Many of her family members joined her there.

Sadly, Harriet was unable to save everyone in her family before slavery was abolished. She was unable to rescue her older sister, Rachel, and her

sister's children, Ben and Angerine. But Harriet was thankful for every loved one she *did* save.

After slavery ended, many Southern states created new laws, called **Black Codes**, to limit the rights of former slaves. Harriet saw how these laws made it hard for her people to find work or health care. Many black people were still poor, and others became very sick.

Harriet saw all black people as her brothers and sisters. She turned her home into a **boardinghouse** to provide food and shelter for those in need. Harriet met her second husband,

## MYTH & FACT

**MYTH:** Life was easy for black people when slavery ended.

**FACT:** Black people still suffered after slavery. It would take almost 100 years for them to be granted equal rights under the Civil Rights Act of 1964.

**JUMP IN THE THINK TANK**

Why do you think life was so hard for enslaved people once they were granted freedom? Remember, they had formerly lived on plantations as the property of their owners.

Nelson Davis, when he stayed at her boardinghouse. They married in 1869, and, together, they ran a farm and a brick business. In 1874, they adopted a daughter, Gertie.

Taking care of other people was expensive. Harriet had served in the Civil War, but the military didn't pay her as they had promised. She had to use money from her farm and business to run her boardinghouse. Later, when Harriet was paid for two biographies written about her life, she knew exactly what she would do with the money.

## A Home for the Poor

Harriet dreamed of creating a home and hospital for poor people, who at that time were called "**indigent**." Soon, she had enough money to buy the land across the street from her house. There, she built the Tubman Home for the Aged and Indigent. Harriet grew vegetables on her farm to feed the poor people who lived at the Tubman Home.

Harriet also earned money for the Tubman Home by giving talks about women's rights. Formerly enslaved black people had limited rights. During this time, women also had few rights and were not allowed to vote. Just as Harriet had spoken about ending slavery, she now spoke to help women get the right to vote.

As more people learned about Harriet's life and her work to help others, she became even more popular. Around 1897, Harriet received from Queen Victoria of England a letter and a gift—a shawl made of white silk lace and linen.

"I was the **conductor** of the Underground Railroad for **eight** years, and I can say what most conductors can't say—I **never** ran my train off the track and **I never lost a passenger.**"

When Harriet became too old and frail to work, she gave her properties to her church, the African Methodist Episcopal Zion Church. Harriet knew her church would continue the important work she began. Harriet died on March 10, 1913. Her amazing life story will be forever loved and respected in American history.

## WHEN?

Harriet marries Nelson Davis. **1869**

Harriet builds the Tubman Home for the Aged and Indigent. **1896**

The Tubman Home accepts its first patients. **1908**

Harriet Tubman dies of pneumonia on March 10. **1913**

# CHAPTER 8

# SO . . . WHO WAS HARRIET TUBMAN?

## Challenge Accepted!

Now that you have learned all about Harriet Tubman's amazing and courageous life, let's check your knowledge with the following quiz. You can look back in the text to find the answers, but try to remember them first!

**1. WHO was Harriet known as when she was a child?**

- A Gertie
- B Minty
- C Little Harriet
- D Miss Sarah

**2. WHAT state granted Harriet her freedom when she ran away from the Poplar Neck Plantation?**

- A Maryland
- B Virginia
- C Pennsylvania
- D New York

**3. WHEN was slavery abolished?**

→ A 1811

→ B 1842

→ C 1860

→ D 1865

**4. WHERE did Harriet buy a house for her family and build a home for the poor?**

→ A Troy, New York

→ B Auburn, New York

→ C St. Catharines, Ontario

→ D Baltimore, Maryland

**5. WHY was Harriet considered a hero?**

→ A She risked her life to help free enslaved people.

→ B She served as a spy and soldier in the American Civil War.

→ C She was an abolitionist.

→ D All of the above.

**6. HOW did Harriet help other enslaved people gain their freedom?**

→ A She used the Underground Railroad.

→ B She purchased their freedom.

→ C She asked slave owners to give them their freedom.

→ D She gave them a map and route to escape.

**7. HOW did runaways know some houses were safe along the secret route of the Underground Railroad?**

→ A Some safe houses were marked on the map with an "X."

→ B Some safe houses had lit lanterns outside.

→ C Some safe houses had red doors.

→ D Some safe houses had blue doors.

**8. WHAT law did Congress pass in 1850 that made Harriet's work even more dangerous?**

→ A The Fugitive Slave Runaway Law

→ B The Reward for Harriet's Capture

→ C The 1850 Law to Capture Runaway Slaves

→ D The Fugitive Slave Law of 1850

**9.** **WHAT laws did Southern states pass after slavery ended that continued to make life difficult for black people?**

→ A Black Laws
→ B Black Rules
→ C Black Codes
→ D Black Regulations

**10.** **WHO was the only sibling Harriet was unable to rescue?**

→ A Rachel
→ B Ben
→ C Henry
→ D Mariah

**Answer Key:** 1. B; 2. C; 3. D; 4. B; 5. D; 6. A; 7. B; 8. D; 9. C; 10. A

## Our World

How has Harriet's work changed our world? Consider a few things that have happened because of Harriet Tubman:

→ Harriet helped people understand the horrors of slavery by giving speeches and lectures about her experience.

→ Harriet led by example, showing how important it is to be an **activist** and **advocate** for the less fortunate.

→ Harriet spoke out on the need for black people and women to have equal rights, including the right to vote.

# JUMP IN THE THINK TANK FOR MORE!

Now let's think a little more about what Harriet Tubman did, how she changed the ways people viewed slavery and women, and how her actions affected our world.

- → Do you think Harriet cared about her popularity or just helping others?
- → Can you imagine how awful life would be for black people if slavery had not been abolished?
- → What if Harriet had only freed herself? How many generations of families would not exist today?

→ If you had the money, would you have opened a home for the sick and poor?

→ Do you think Harriet ever imagined that her life would inspire others?

The Harriet Tubman Home for the Aged and Indigent

# Glossary

**abolish:** to put an end to something, such as a law, policy, or practice

**abolitionist:** a person who favors abolishing something or agrees to abolish something, such as a law, policy, or practice

**activist:** a person who takes action for or against something

**advocate:** a person who defends or supports a cause or person

**ancestry:** a person's parents, grandparents, and other relatives going back into history

**Black Codes:** laws that were passed after slavery was abolished; laws that limited the rights and freedoms of black people

**boardinghouse:** a place where people can stay overnight and where food is served

**bounty:** money paid for the capture, or killing, or both of a person or animal

**conductor:** a person in charge of a train or a streetcar transportation system

**descendant:** a child, grandchild, great-grandchild, and so on

**disguises:** clothing worn to change one's appearance so as to be unrecognizable

**enslaved:** forced into slavery

**enslaved people:** people forced into slavery; also known as slaves

**harvesting:** the process of gathering crops

**indigent:** poor (outdated)

**liaison:** a person who helps two groups of people communicate

**overseer:** a person who supervised the work of slaves on a plantation

**plantation:** an estate that uses manual labor to take care of crops and agriculture such as cotton, tobacco, and sugar

**privileges:** special rights, opportunities, or both that are given only to certain people, not everyone

**Quaker:** a person who is a member of the Religious Society of Friends, a Christian movement founded by George Fox in 1650; members are devoted to peaceful principles and practices

**rebellion:** the act of going against an authority

**slave:** a person forced to work in slavery; also known as an enslaved person

**slave owners:** people who enslaved other people and treated them like property

**slavery:** a system in which people are treated like property and forced to work for no wages

**terrain:** a stretch of land, often with specific characteristics

# Bibliography

Bradford, Sarah Hopkins. *Harriet, The Moses of Her People*. New York: George R. Lockwood and Son, 1886.

Gold, Susan Dudley. *Harriet Tubman and the Underground Railroad*. New York: Cavendish Square Publishing, 2016.

McMillian, Angela. *Harriet Tubman: A Resource Guide*. Library of Congress (2019).

# Acknowledgments

Without Quaker abolitionist Levi Coffin, who was known as the "President of the Underground Railroad," and other brave men and women who risked their lives to help enslaved people escape to freedom, thousands of former slaves and their descendants would never have survived. Mr. Coffin's house was known as "grand central station" because so many runaway slaves found safety there. Countless other enslaved blacks, freed blacks, and white supporters helped guide numerous people to the North and Canada. May their work remind and encourage us to always do what we can to help those in need. —CP

# About the Author

**Christine Platt** is a passionate advocate for social justice and policy reform. She holds a B.A. in Africana Studies from the University of South Florida, an M.A. in African and African American Studies from The Ohio State University, and a J.D. from Stetson University College of Law. A believer in the power of storytelling as a tool for social change, Christine teaches people of all ages about race, equity, diversity, and inclusion.

# About the Illustrator

Based in Los Angeles, **Loris Lora** is a multidisciplinary artist who has worked in editorial publishing, book publishing, children's toy design, and surface design. She has been featured in galleries across the globe. Her attention to detail and eye for color helps inform her creative voice. Her style is largely inspired by mid-century design, pop culture, and her Mexican upbringing. Her sensitive and insightful portraiture conveys complex concepts and narratives with delicate humor and an engaging humanity. Her digital work is as vibrant as her gouache images.